STORIES
WELL TOLD

PUBLISHED *by* Creative Education
P.O. Box 227, Mankato, Minnesota 56002
Creative Education is an imprint of The Creative Company
www.thecreativecompany.us

DESIGN AND PRODUCTION *by* Ellen Huber
ART DIRECTION *by* Rita Marshall
PRINTED *in the* United States of America

PHOTOGRAPHS *by*
Alamy (AF archive, INTERFOTO, Mary Evans Picture Library,
Moviestore collection Ltd, Pictorial Press Ltd, The Print Collector),
Dreamstime (Mega11), Getty Images (20th Century-Fox, Larry Ellis/Express,
John Kobal Foundation, David Montgomery, Oliver Morris, Popperfoto,
Time & Life Pictures), Mary Evans Picture Library (WALT DISNEY
PICTURES/Ronald Grant Archive), Newscom (Toronto Star/ZUMA Press,
UNIVERSAL PICTURES), Shutterstock (DarkGeometryStudios,
Johnna Evang Nonboe, sad, sgame), Veer (Ocean Illustration)

Library of Congress Cataloging-in-Publication Data
Bodden, Valerie.
Science fiction / Valerie Bodden.
p. cm. — (Stories well told)
Includes bibliographical references and index.
*Summary: A survey of the science fiction genre, from its Industrial
Revolution-era origins and technological influences to the famous authors—such
as Jules Verne—whose works have defined the genre over time.*

ISBN 978-1-60818-181-0
1. Science fiction—History and criticism—Juvenile literature. I. Title.

PN3433.5.B59 2012
809.3'8762—dc23   2012023237

First Edition
2 4 6 8 9 7 5 3 1

VALERIE BODDEN

SCIENCE FICTION

CREATIVE ● EDUCATION

TABLE OF CONTENTS

JULES VERNE SITS IN HIS LIBRARY, A NUMBER OF BOOKS AND JOURNALS OPEN ON THE LARGE DESK IN FRONT OF HIM.

———◆———

Some are physics texts, others describe the newly discovered wonders of the oceans, and still others detail the wildlife of the African plains. Pulling a physics book closer, Verne studies formulas, jots down figures, and reworks numbers. Finally, he has it: the calculations that will send a man to the moon! Verne doesn't rush off to find an astronaut, though. Instead, he picks up a manuscript and begins to write. The man he plans to send to the moon is a fictional character in one of his books, but that doesn't matter to the prolific author. He wants to be sure that the facts in his Extraordinary Voyages stories are as accurate as if they described a real-life journey. Perhaps someday, he reasons, such flights of fancy may come true.

Science fiction has its roots in fantasy, a genre of literature that features imaginary worlds, the supernatural, and magic. Whereas fantasy offers no logical explanations for its fantastic elements, science fiction relies on science—whether real or imagined—to explain why the conditions or setting of a story differ from that of the world we know. It often centers on the scientific discoveries, theories, and ideas of its time.

Although the first true science fiction stories did not appear until the 19th century, a number of earlier works foreshadowed the eventual development of the genre. As early as the second century A.D., the Greek writer Lucian, in his book *True History*, described a trip to the moon in which the protagonist is taken to the heavenly body in a whirlwind. In German astronomer Johannes Kepler's *Somnium* (1634), the hero of the tale uses witchcraft to get to the moon—but the setting aligns with scientific descriptions of the moon's surface. Other early stories featured journeys into the center of the earth or into the future. In most cases, however, the focus of these stories was political satire or humor, and the authors paid little attention to plausible explanations or descriptions of the science involved.

During the 19th century, the rapid development of science and the rise of technology through the Industrial Revolution gave authors a new focus, and the science fiction genre began to emerge. Many scholars consider British author Mary Wollstonecraft Shelley's novel *Frankenstein; or, The Modern Prometheus* (1818) as the first-ever work of science fiction, as it depicts a scientist who uses electricity to bring to life a creature of his own making. Early credit for the development of science fiction has also been given to American author Edgar Allan Poe. In his short story "The Unparalleled Adventure of One Hans Phaall" (1835), the protagonist describes in detail his journey to the moon in a balloon, including the technology he used to breathe in space: "I had prepared a very strong perfectly

< 8 >

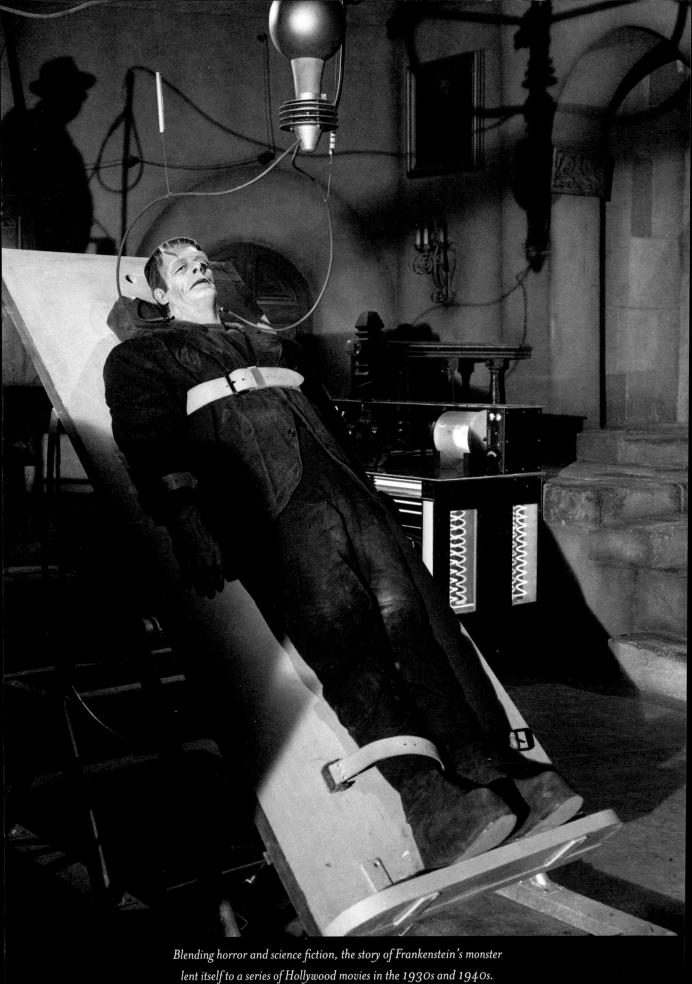

*Blending horror and science fiction, the story of Frankenstein's monster
lent itself to a series of Hollywood movies in the 1930s and 1940s.*

A key element of much of science fiction is imagining what futuristic cities—
even those on other planets—might look like and how they would be built.

air-tight, but flexible gum-elastic bag. In this bag,... the entire car was in a manner placed.... Through [a] tube a quantity of the rare atmosphere ... was thence discharged ... to mingle with the thin air already in the chamber." Such scientific descriptions gave Poe's work what is called verisimilitude, or a feeling of truth, a quality that would be adopted by later science fiction writers.

While the works of Shelley and Poe are often considered forerunners of science fiction, French author Jules Verne and British author H. G. Wells exerted even greater influence on the developing genre and are regarded by many as the true fathers of modern science fiction. In a number of science-adventure stories, Verne turned the focus of science fiction toward the creation of new "gadgets," such as submarines, and the scientific discoveries that could be made with them. Although Wells's science fiction also featured scientific backgrounds, he used his stories as a platform for delivering social commentary, a hallmark that would come to characterize many future works in the genre.

By the late 19th century, many works of science fiction had begun to appear across Europe and in the United States. Reflecting a sense of optimism about the future, a number of stories explored the idea of utopia, or the establishment of a perfect state. In some, such as American coach-builder and author Chauncey Thomas's *The Crystal Button* (1891), advanced technology created utopian conditions. In the following excerpt from the story, Paul Prognosis questions Professor Prosper about the technology he finds in a utopian city of the 49th century. (Since the book was written in the 1870s, before the invention of the airplane or the widespread use of electricity, such advancements still seemed far-flung.)

> *"These cloud shadows that now and then pass us, are they clouds, or huge birds, or balloons of some kind?"*
>
> *"They are air-ships...."*

< 11 >

A SCIENCE FICTION CHARACTER

For most of its history, science fiction has placed more emphasis on plot, setting, and theme (such as specific moral or social questions) than on character development. In most works, it is not the characters themselves but the situations and events in which they take part that forms the focus, although a number of more recent science fiction works have paid more attention to detailed renderings of their characters.

In much early science fiction, the protagonist of the story was a scientist, such as Dr. Victor Frankenstein in Mary Shelley's **Frankenstein**. In other works, the hero was an engineer or an inventor, such as Dr. Samuel Ferguson in Jules Verne's **Five Weeks in a Balloon**. By the late 19th century, all kinds of scientists—from doctors to archaeologists—were being featured in science fiction stories. Around the 1920s, the protagonist in science fiction works shifted from the scientist to the adventurer. The character Beowulf Shaeffer in Larry Niven's **Known Space** series, for example, is a spaceship pilot who travels to the center of the Milky Way, explores dangerous stars and planets, and undertakes daring rescues. In other works, the protagonist is an average person, much like Winston Smith in George Orwell's **Nineteen Eighty-Four**. In some science fiction works, the protagonist is actually an antihero, lacking the traditional morality, courage, or idealism expected of a hero. Such is the case with Rick Deckard, the bounty hunter of Philip K. Dick's **Do Androids Dream of Electric Sheep?**

BIG BROTHER
IS WATCH
YOU

American actor Edmond
O'Brien played the role of
rebellious clerk Winston Smith
in the first movie
adaptation (released in 1956)
of Orwell's 1984.

"What," asked Paul, "is the purpose of the tall masts that I see scattered so thickly through the city?..."

"These masts are simply supports for electric suns by which we convert darkness into day, so that midnight and noon are scarcely to be distinguished in Tone."

Such descriptions reflected the belief that technological advances would help society progress. Other authors, however, were less optimistic about the benefits and created utopias in which people returned to a simpler, rural way of life.

Rather than looking to fictional locations on Earth as the setting for their works, some authors focused on journeys to the moon or Mars. Still others looked to Earth's future, predicting the use of new, more powerful weapons in wars to come. After World War I (1914–18), much of the science fiction published in England was marked by a pessimistic view of human progress. Instead of utopias, many authors created dystopias, or worlds where political corruption and the misuse of technology resulted in a terrible quality of life.

In contrast, American authors focused on lighter topics such as interplanetary romance and space operas (large-scale adventure stories featuring space travel and alien beings). Most of these stories were published in "pulp" magazines (so called because of the cheap, wood-pulp paper on which they were printed). Among the earliest science fiction pulps was *Amazing Stories*, which published stories deemed to be prophetic, educational, and exciting. In 1937, an American science fiction author named John W. Campbell became editor of the pulp magazine *Astounding Science Fiction*. Most scholars consider this year to mark the beginning of a "Golden Age" for science fiction that lasted into the 1960s. Campbell demanded high-quality literature from his authors and required that stories be based on accurate scientific research. While *Astounding* stories emphasized

< 14 >

Eando Binder's 1939 pulp-magazine short story "I, Robot" inspired
Isaac Asimov's later (and more famous) collection of the same name.

plausible science over adventure, they also often explored relationships between human beings and science.

During and immediately after World War II (1939–45), science fiction authors turned their focus once again to future wars, often predicting the near collapse of human civilization. While some authors began to treat technological advancements more cynically after the war, others embraced the use of technology, portraying robots and other forms of artificial intelligence.

Science fiction underwent a revolution in the 1960s with the advent of the New Wave movement, which sought to transform the genre through experimentation in both form and content. New Wave authors turned away from "hard" science fiction (with emphases on technology and outer space) and moved toward "soft" science fiction (centered on the social sciences). Reflecting the influences of the Vietnam War (1954–75), widespread drug use, and ecological dangers, New Wave works tended to present a bleak picture of the future.

By the 1980s, many authors were looking to the developing world of computers and cyberspace, creating grim, cynical, and often violent stories known as "cyberpunk." In recent years, topics such as biotechnology, alternate history (in which some aspect of history as we know it has been changed), and ecological disaster have come to the forefront of the genre.

The uninterrupted development of science fiction has led to the growth of an ever-expanding audience. Although many science fiction fans begin reading works in the genre during their early teens, a significant number retain this interest for life. And while most science fiction readers were once male, a growing number of women now enjoy works in the genre as well.

< 16 >

lthough most science fiction stories deal with science in some way, works in the genre vary widely and can be divided into a number of subgenres (or sub-categories). When many people think of science fiction, they think of works falling into the hard science fiction category, wherein some scientific principle or idea is at the heart of the story. Hard science fiction authors closely adhere to scientific facts, although they may come up with new theories or extrapolate scientific progress into the future to create technologies or even entire worlds. Soft science fiction, on the other hand, puts more emphasis on social concerns and morality, often examining the effects of science on people and society. Most of the other subgenres of science fiction fit into either the hard or soft science fiction categories—or somewhere in between.

Since the beginnings of the genre, much of science fiction has revolved around space travel. The cosmic voyage subgenre, for example, focuses on journeys through space to other worlds, including to unknown planets outside our solar system or galaxy. Since such trips would necessarily take many light years, science fiction authors have invented "hyperdrives" to allow their spacecraft to travel faster than the speed of light, despite the fact that this is scientifically impossible.

Similar to the cosmic voyage, space operas take place in outer space and on faraway planets. These epic stories often span thousands of years and vast expanses of the universe. Their action-packed plots follow the heroes as they fight to vanquish evil against overwhelming odds. Although writer and director George Lucas's *Star Wars* films are probably the most popular space opera of all time, newer works in the genre attract many fans and regularly win science fiction awards.

Closely related to—and often overlapping with—stories of space adventure are works of the alien civilization subgenre. In early works, aliens were often described as friendly beings similar to humans. But in 1898, H. G. Wells introduced the idea

< 17 >

In The War of the Worlds, *Wells describes the Martians'*
three-legged combat machines as "walking engine[s] of glittering metal."

of hostile aliens in *The War of the Worlds*, a novel that depicts the invasion of Earth by Martians who wish to kill and enslave human beings. As the narrator describes them, the aliens are repulsive: "A big greyish rounded bulk, the size, perhaps, of a bear.... It glistened like wet leather. Two large dark-coloured eyes were regarding me steadfastly. The mass that framed them, the head of the thing, was rounded, and had, one might say, a face. There was a mouth under the eyes, the lipless brim of which quivered and panted, and dropped saliva. The whole creature heaved and pulsated convulsively. A lank tentacular appendage [tentacle] gripped the edge of the cylinder, another swayed in the air. Those who have never seen a living Martian can scarcely imagine the strange horror of its appearance." Later authors created alien creatures that could not be judged by human standards; they were not necessarily good or bad, but simply different.

Not all nonhuman life in science fiction is alien. The artificial intelligence subgenre features intelligent machines that have been created by humans, including computers, robots, and androids (artificial humans). In many cases, androids are made nearly indistinguishable from human beings, raising questions about the definition of humanity. In American author Philip K. Dick's *Do Androids Dream of Electric Sheep?* (1968), the protagonist Rick Deckard discusses with the android Garland one of the primary differences between human and artificial life:

> *"You androids," Rick said, "don't exactly cover for each other in times of stress."*

> *Garland snapped, "I think you're right; it would seem we lack a specific talent you humans possess. I believe it's called empathy."*

On another occasion, Deckard is struck by the lack of emotion a female android displays: "A topic of world-shaking importance, yet dealt with facetiously [humorously]; an android trait, possibly, he thought. No emotional awareness,

< 19 >

A SCIENCE FICTION ACTIVITY

In order to get a better feel for the different subgenres of science fiction, it can be helpful to look at works that fall into several categories. Pick out three or four science fiction works representing different subgenres (Jules Verne's From the Earth to the Moon for hard science fiction, H. G. Wells's The Time Machine for time travel or The War of the Worlds for alien invasion, E. E. Smith's Galactic Patrol for space opera, and Ray Bradbury's Fahrenheit 451 for dystopia, for example). Read several pages of each work, making note of the characteristics that qualify it for the specific subgenre into which it is most often categorized. Do you see any elements of other subgenres in the work as well? Which fictional world do you find the most plausible? Which is the most fantastic? Which do you like the best?

Now, try your hand at writing some science fiction of your own. Imagine that you have been transported into the world of one of these works. Tell your reader how you got there (this is science fiction, after all). What do you see around you? How do you react? Is there any technology worth noting? What about social conditions? Will you stay to explore or to settle, or will you jump on the next ship out of that world? When you've finished writing, show your work to your friends or family. How do they feel about your adventures in science fiction?

Wells invented the term "time machine," and such a vehicle has been used in science fiction stories—appearing in many forms—ever since.

E.T.
THE EXTRA-TERRESTRIAL

The 1982 film E.T. is the story of a boy who befriends an alien,
which isn't the typical plot of an alien civilization/invasion science fiction tale.

no feeling-sense of the actual *meaning* of what she said. Only the hollow, formal, intellectual definitions of the separate terms." Thus, Dick emphasizes that to be human means not only to exist and to think but also to feel.

Other subgenres of science fiction include those that present alternate worlds or alternate histories, in which events from the past are changed to present intriguing "what if?" scenarios. Such works might examine what life would be like if Christopher Columbus had not traveled to America, for example. Conversely, other subgenres, such as the apocalyptic, look to the future. Apocalyptic stories examine the end of the world as we know it, which is often achieved through nuclear war. Branching off from apocalyptic stories is the post-apocalypse subgenre, which examines the conditions on Earth after an apocalyptic disaster. While alternate history and apocalyptic fiction are set in either the past or the future, works in the time travel subgenre feature characters who can bridge both, traveling back and forth through time with the aid of devices or technologies.

Even tales of superheroes fall into a subgenre of science fiction: the "superbeing" subgenre, which presumes that selected individuals develop greater physical or mental abilities than other individuals in a certain species. In *More than Human* (1953) by American author Theodore Sturgeon (pen name of Edward Hamilton Waldo), for example, six characters with powers ranging from telepathy (mind-reading) to telekinesis (using the mind to move objects) fuse their skills to become one superhuman organism. In many cases, such stories deal with the problems, as well as the advantages, associated with these new traits.

Some subgenres of science fiction are meant to appeal to specific audiences. Feminist science fiction, for example, deals with women's issues, featuring stories about women's roles, gender wars, or female utopias. Juvenile science fiction addresses a younger audience and often features teenaged protagonists, as in American

< 23 >

author William Sleator's *Interstellar Pig* (1984), which features 16-year-old Barney and his discovery of a board game that he must win to prevent Earth's destruction.

Although the various science fiction subgenres are most often treated in novels today, short stories—especially those published in pulp magazines—have historically been the backbone of the genre. Among the pulp stories is Stanley G. Weinbaum's "The Lotus Eaters" (1935). Known for creating fantastic worlds, Weinbaum in this story describes an intelligent species of mobile plants encountered on the dark side of Venus. Explorers Pat and Ham Hammond are surprised to learn that the plants, which they call "Oscar," have no survival instinct:

> *"But Oscar, why—why don't you use your knowledge to protect yourselves from your enemies?"*
>
> *"There is no need. There is no need to do anything. In a hundred years we shall be—"* Silence.
>
> *"Safe?"*
>
> *"Yes—no."*
>
> *"What?"* A horrible thought struck her. *"Do you mean—extinct?"*
>
> *"Yes."*
>
> *"But—oh, Oscar! Don't you want to live? Don't your people want to survive?"*
>
> *"Want,"* shrilled Oscar. *"Want—want—want. That word means nothing."*
>
> *"It means—it means desire, need."*
>
> *"Desire means nothing. Need—need. No. My people do not need to survive."*

New science fiction short stories continue to be published today as well, often in anthologies, or collections, which may feature works by a single author or about a single subject. Each year, a number of publishers also release anthologies of what they have determined to be the best short science fiction of the year, thereby helping to set the standard for future works in the genre.

< 24 >

New worlds with imaginative landscapes are constantly being fashioned

When Mary Shelley wrote *Frankenstein* at the age of 18, she did not set out to create a work of science fiction, but the novel is today considered by many scholars to be the first novel in that genre. While the central focus of the work is more philosophical than scientific, the story does revolve around a scientist named Victor Frankenstein (although he is not termed a scientist, since that word was not invented until 1834). Frankenstein has found a way to give life to something inanimate by means of a kind of electricity called galvanism. Such an idea reflected the science of Shelley's time, which she had discussed with her husband, poet Percy Bysshe Shelley, and fellow British poet Lord Byron. Although the scientific principles are only vaguely described, Dr. Frankenstein relates the culmination of his work: "I collected the instruments of life around me, that I might infuse a spark of being into the lifeless thing that lay at my feet.... I saw the dull yellow eye of the creature open; it breathed hard, and a convulsive motion agitated its limbs." Far from being elated with his creation, Dr. Frankenstein rejects it, and the creature in turn becomes vengeful, killing everyone close to its creator. In her portrayal of Frankenstein's monster, Shelley demonstrated the potential dangers and pitfalls of scientific achievement, a theme that would be taken up by many science fiction authors in the years to come.

Jules Verne's first science fiction novel, *Five Weeks in a Balloon* (1863), actually began life as a nonfiction article about the possibilities of balloon travel in Africa. At his publisher's request, Verne turned the article into a fictional story in which the protagonist floats across Africa in a balloon, meeting with a number of adventures along the way. The tale became the first in a series known as The Extraordinary Voyages, which also included *Journey to the Center of the Earth* (1864), *From the Earth to the Moon* (1865), and *Twenty Thousand Leagues Under the Sea*

< 26 >

Verne's **Five Weeks in a Balloon** *came to the silver screen in 1962,*

The vessel in Twenty Thousand Leagues Under the Sea, *the* Nautilus, *was named after inventor Robert Fulton's early successful submarine from 1800.*

(1870). In these works, Verne combined a boyhood love of exploration with a celebration of science, imparting real facts to his readers and often predicting the technological developments of the future. In *Twenty Thousand Leagues Under the Sea*, for example, Verne's protagonist travels in a submarine called the *Nautilus*, the electrical workings of which are described in detail. At the same time, the narrator provides an introduction to oceanography: "The sea has its large rivers like the continents. They are special currents known by their temperature and their color…. Science has decided on the globe the direction of five principal currents." Verne's works exerted a major influence on the genre, especially in the realm of hard science fiction.

American author Edgar Rice Burroughs (best known as the creator of Tarzan) turned to writing only after failing at a number of other careers. In writing he found success, ushering in a new type of science fiction that shifted the focus away from science and toward interplanetary adventure and romance. In his first work, serialized in the pulps as *Under the Moons of Mars* (1912) and later published as the novel *A Princess of Mars* (1917), Burroughs paid little attention to the technology needed to get his hero, John Carter, to Mars. Instead, Carter finds himself suddenly transported to that planet from an Arizona cave. Once there, he meets ferocious green Martians and saves a red Martian princess, who looks much like a human but has light red skin. Burroughs went on to write 10 more novels set on Mars, as well as a series about Pellucidar, a world found at the center of a hollow Earth, and works set on Venus and the moon. In each tale, action, swordplay, suspense, and romance take center stage, rather than science. As a result, many critics have categorized his works as science fantasy (a combination of science fiction and fantasy). Nevertheless, Burroughs's tremendously popular stories helped focus the direction of American pulp fiction in the following years.

< 29 >

A SCIENCE FICTION MASTER

Born in England in 1866, H. G. Wells grew up in a poverty-stricken family. After winning a college scholarship, he became a science teacher before turning to writing. By the time he died in 1946, Wells had written numerous works of science fiction, eventually earning a reputation as one of the founders and most influential authors of the genre.

Although Wells often included scientific principles in his works, in most cases, the science forms a backdrop for examining larger social issues. The Time Machine *(1895), for example, presents the first fictional machine for moving people through time, but its focus is on what the protagonist, called simply the Time Traveller, finds when he travels to the year* A.D. *802,701. Earth has been divided into two subspecies of humans: the leisurely, inactive Eloi and the hardworking, ape-like Morlocks, who feed on the Eloi. From this point, the Time Traveller jumps farther into the future, where he sees the dying Earth: "The world was silent.... All the sounds of man, the bleating of sheep, the cries of birds, the hum of insects, the stir that makes the background of our lives—all that was over." The pessimistic mood of* The Time Machine *was reflected in a number of Wells's other early works, including* The Island of Dr. Moreau *(1896),* The Invisible Man *(1897), and* The War of the Worlds *(1898). In 1905, however, Wells published* A Modern Utopia, *a novel demonstrating his hope of social progress. Toward the end of his life, though, Wells largely returned to his earlier pessimistic outlook.*

H. G. Wells did not restrict his writing to science fiction but also authored novels set in his own time, historical works, and political commentaries.

Even as epic stories of space adventure in the Burroughs style flourished in America, many writers in Britain turned to darker subjects after World War I. Aldous Huxley published the dystopian novel *Brave New World* in 1932 as a reflection of his own distrust of the technological advances and political systems of his day. In the book, the World State government uses technology—including drugs that induce happiness—to control its global citizens, most of whom are eager to follow its rules. In this world, where the motto is "Community, Identity, Stability," citizens are taught to believe that "when the individual feels, the community reels." Those who do not follow the rules are banished or die. Huxley's other works, such as *After Many a Summer Dies the Swan* (1939), in which humans prove to be lesser-developed apes, contain similar social criticism.

In America, meanwhile, the prolific author Robert Heinlein, who had studied mathematics and physics at the University of California, managed to blend hard science fiction with social and political concerns. Claiming to be influenced by everything he had ever "seen, touched, eaten, endured, heard, and read," Heinlein created stories grounded in reality, picturing a plausible future in which human beings could do things once considered impossible. Heinlein's career was launched in the pages of the magazine *Astounding*, where he published a number of stories under both his own name and pseudonyms (made-up names). He also wrote more than 30 novels, including *Starship Troopers* (1959) and *Stranger in a Strange Land* (1961). The first describes a war against an alien race, while the second focuses on the return to Earth of a human who has been raised and educated by Martians. Heinlein's sophisticated writing style raised the standard for literary quality in science fiction.

Like many science fiction authors of the mid-20th century, British writer Arthur C. Clarke first discovered the genre in the pages of the American pulps.

< 32 >

BRAVE NEW WORLD

Huxley's Brave New World *turned a critical eye on the utopian views
of popular science fiction authors of his time such as H.G. Wells.*

Clarke's 1951 short story "The Sentinel" served as the seed of inspiration for the film and companion novel 2001: A Space Odyssey.

After earning degrees in physics and mathematics, Clarke published his first successful novel, *Childhood's End* (1953). The book describes the arrival on Earth of a superior alien species that teaches human beings to leave the planet—and their bodies—to join a galactic "spirit" called the Overmind. In many of his other works, Clarke questioned human beings' readiness to handle the consequences of their scientific discoveries. Among his best-known works is *2001: A Space Odyssey* (1968), which he wrote as both a novel and a film with director Stanley Kubrick. The work features a computer that attempts to kill the crew of a spacecraft. After disconnecting the computer, the protagonist, Dr. David Bowman, completes his journey and eventually becomes a Star Child, capable of living and traveling in space forever. Both the movie and the novel were highly acclaimed, prompting one critic to declare them a "science fiction milestone—one of the best novels in the genre and undoubtedly the best SF [science fiction] movie ever made." Like *2001: A Space Odyssey*, many of Clarke's works charmed readers with their combination of hard scientific fact and an expression of wonder toward the mysteries of the universe.

< 35 >

With a doctorate in biochemistry, American author Isaac Asimov was well-versed in science, and many of his nearly 500 written works are nonfiction pieces explaining scientific topics, including chemistry, energy, and space. He also wrote some of the most popular science fiction stories of the 20th century, including the Foundation trilogy. Based loosely on the fall of the Roman Empire, the series chronicles the history of a vast galactic empire. Scientists in the empire use psychohistory (an invented science that uses mathematics to predict the future) to determine that their civilization will soon collapse into a dark age. But they have developed a plan that will shorten that dark age, as long as the empire's citizens cooperate, as the creator of psychohistory explains to them: "From now on, and into the centuries, the path you must take is inevitable. You will be faced with a series of crises,… and in each case your freedom of action will become similarly circumscribed [limited] so that you will be forced along one, and only one, path." Along with his Foundation trilogy, Asimov is best known for *I, Robot* (1950), a collection of related short stories that presents the "Laws of Robotics": robots may not injure a human, they must obey a human's orders, and they must protect themselves. These laws have been adopted in countless stories about robots published since the 1950s.

Beginning his writing career around the same time as Asimov, American author Ray Bradbury published a number of pulp stories, along with short-story collections such as *The Martian Chronicles* (1950). Regarded today as a classic in the genre, the book recounts the settlement of Mars by humans, who plunder and exploit the peaceful Martian world. In a story called "The Off Season," a settler from Earth named Sam Parkhill confronts a native Martian with hostility:

> *"I thought I told you I don't want you near here!" cried Sam. "Go on, I'll give you the Disease!"*

< 36 >

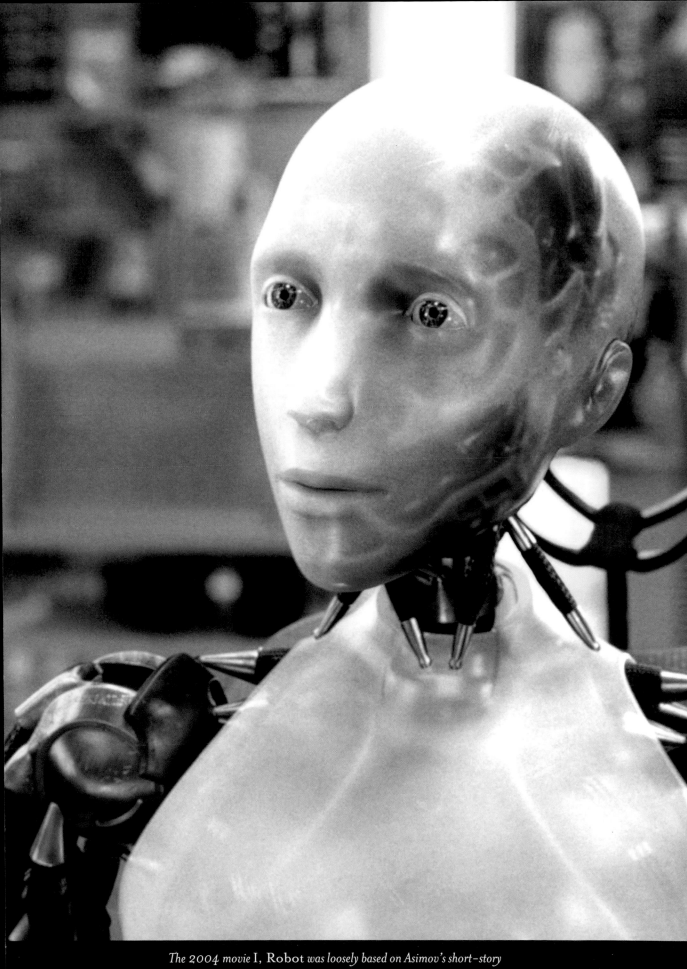

The 2004 movie I, Robot *was loosely based on Asimov's short-story collection of the same name and featured a robot called Sonny.*

*In one of his books, Kurt Vonnegut grades his own work, giving the
highest marks to the novels* Cat's Cradle *and* Slaughterhouse-Five.

"I've already had the Disease," said the voice [of the Martian]. "I was one of the few survivors. I was sick a long time."

"Go on and hide in the hills, that's where you belong...."

"We mean you no harm."

"But I mean you harm!" said Sam, backing up. "I don't like strangers. I don't like Martians. I never seen one before. It ain't natural."

In addition to his numerous short stories, Bradbury also wrote several novels, including the dystopia *Fahrenheit 451* (1953). The protagonist of this story, Guy Montag, is a fireman who burns books banned by the government, which wants to prevent people from thinking freely. Lauded for his sophisticated prose and poetic style, Bradbury is still widely read by both science fiction fans and readers of mainstream fiction.

Like Bradbury, American author Kurt Vonnegut's works have been widely accepted and acclaimed, even outside science fiction circles. Taking an even more pessimistic view than Bradbury, Vonnegut used the techniques of science fiction to create works bitingly critical of modern society, war, technology, government, and religion. His first novel, *Player Piano* (1952), for example, depicts a group of scientists who unsuccessfully attempt to achieve a meaningful life in their society, which is largely run by machines. Vonnegut's most famous work, *Slaughterhouse-Five; or, The Children's Crusade: A Duty-Dance with Death* (1969), pictures the World War II bombing of the city of Dresden, Germany (which Vonnegut experienced personally as a prisoner of war), and its effects on the story's protagonist, Billy Pilgrim.

Despite Vonnegut's emphasis on soft science fiction, many authors continued to create works based on hard scientific principles. American author

< 39 >

A SCIENCE FICTION CLASSIC

Published in 1949, British author George Orwell's (pseudonym of Eric Arthur Blair) dystopia Nineteen Eighty-Four has become one of the best known of all science fiction works. The novel is set in the totalitarian superstate of Oceania, which encompasses Airstrip One (based on real-life England) and a number of other areas. The leader of Oceania, Big Brother, rules by means of thought control, brainwashing, and propaganda. Every action of Oceania's citizens is captured by video surveillance, as huge signs remind them: "The poster with the enormous face gazed from the wall. It was one of those pictures which are so contrived that the eyes follow you about when you move. BIG BROTHER IS WATCHING YOU, the caption beneath it ran." The story's protagonist, Winston Smith, works in the Ministry of Truth, rewriting history for Oceania. But, wanting to feel human, Winston rebels, keeping a secret diary and conducting an affair with a coworker. Ultimately, his rebellion is unsuccessful; after being tortured, he is reeducated and in the end realizes, "He had won the victory over himself. He loved Big Brother."

Ultimately, the novel serves as a critique of—and warning against—totalitarianism and attacks on human freedom. In this, it helped to usher in a mode of science fiction focusing on social concerns. A measure of the work's influence lies in the many words coined by Orwell that have become a part of everyday language, including "Big Brother" (a dictator who maintains constant surveillance), "doublethink" (holding two contradictory beliefs at the same time), and "newspeak" (language that hides the truth).

In a scene from a 1965
television production of 1984,
Winston Smith is tortured
by O'Brien, a member
of the Inner Party,
the ruling upper class.

Poul Anderson, for example, studied physics at the University of Minnesota and incorporated what he learned there into his writing. His most successful novel, *Tau Zero* (1970), portrays a spaceship that is accelerating out of control, approaching the speed of light. Using the special theory of relativity developed by Albert Einstein, Anderson shows how time inside the craft remains at its normal pace, while outside it, time quickens to the point that millions of years pass by in a matter of seconds.

In his early works, British author J. G. Ballard also embraced hard science fiction, but in the mid-1960s, he turned to a more experimental style and subject matter—the "inner space" of the human mind—to become one of the most important writers of the New Wave movement. Ballard's stark, apocalyptic worlds were highly influenced by the two years he spent in a Japanese internment camp as a teenager living in China during World War II. In many cases, his works show how humans must adapt in order to survive ecological devastation caused by the effects of technology. In *The Crystal World* (1966), for example, the African rainforest is becoming crystallized by a strange phenomenon. The novel's opening demonstrates Ballard's rich imagery: "Above all, the darkness of the river was what impressed Dr. Sanders.... Although it was ten o'clock the surface of the water was still gray and sluggish.... At intervals, when the sky was overcast, the water was almost black, like putrescent [rotting] dye." Although the New Wave movement ended by the late 1970s, Ballard's style proved highly influential to the science fiction writers who followed him and helped to expand the realm of soft science fiction.

Like Ballard, American author Ursula K. Le Guin wrote New Wave works (in addition to works in other genres, including fantasy) acclaimed for their literary style. In a genre dominated by men, Le Guin is credited with helping to bring feminist themes to the foreground. *The Left Hand of Darkness* (1969), for

< 42 >

*Ballard became familiar with American science fiction stories
while training with Great Britain's Royal Air Force in Canada in 1953.*

Gibson's Neuromancer *was the first book in his Sprawl trilogy,*
which continued with Count Zero *in 1986 and* Mona Lisa Overdrive *in 1988.*

instance, pictures a society in which humans are neither male nor female, except once a month, when they can take on the characteristics of either sex. Another novel, *The Dispossessed* (1974), explores moral and political issues in conjunction with its description of a flawed utopia.

Tired of what he termed "stodgy [boring] and geeked-out" science fiction, American-Canadian author William Gibson became the leader of the cyberpunk movement with his 1984 novel *Neuromancer*. The work's protagonist is the antihero Henry Dorsett Case, a hacker in cyberspace (a term coined by Gibson). Case and the other characters in the novel have the ability to connect their minds directly to the virtual world. This fast-paced, dark story, enmeshed in drugs, murder, and intrigue, set off a literary firestorm and inspired numerous works in the subgenre over the following decade.

Today, a number of writers continue to push the science fiction genre forward. Among them is Tim Powers, an American author whose "secret histories" fuse science fiction and fantasy to reveal the supernatural forces that have influenced historical people and events. Scottish writer Iain M. Banks, meanwhile, addresses social issues with his series of novels based on The Culture, a utopian society in which possessions, disease, and inequality have been almost eliminated.

Like science itself, science fiction has changed and developed since its beginnings in the 19th century. From an emphasis on hard scientific fact to romps through space and examinations of human society, science fiction has provided a forum for exploring both life as we know it and as we imagine it to be. As the hard and soft sciences continue to advance, so, too, does science fiction, with its speculations on the developments yet to come—and how humans will react to and write about them.

< 45 >

antihero: the main character of a story who lacks traditional heroic qualities, such as moral integrity or bravery

archaeologists: people who study ancient societies by examining what they left behind, such as buildings, records, and tools

biotechnology: the use of engineering and technology on living organisms

ecological: having to do with the environment and the interactions of living organisms with their surroundings

extrapolate: to use known facts to come to conclusions about something unknown by assuming that certain conditions will remain the same

galaxy: a large group of stars, planets, and dust that is held together by gravity

genre: a category in which a literary work can be classified on the basis of style, technique, or subject matter

Industrial Revolution: a period during the late 18th and early 19th centuries in Great Britain, Europe, and the U.S., marked by a shift from economies based on agriculture to ones based on mechanized production in factories

internment: the imprisonment or confinement of a group of people for political reasons

light years: units of distance describing how far light travels in a vacuum (empty, airless space) in one year

oceanography: the study of the water, life, and resources of the oceans

physics: the study of forces, energy, and motion

plausible: believable and seemingly true

protagonist: the main character in a work of fiction

satire: the use of ridicule or sarcasm to criticize or expose human folly or vice

serialized: published in parts

social sciences: scientific studies of human society and relationships, including the fields of psychology, sociology, and history

solar system: a group of planets orbiting a star

special theory of relativity: a scientific theory dealing with the relationship between time, space, and matter

supernatural: relating to objects or powers that have no natural explanation and seem to exist outside natural laws

totalitarian: having to do with a government that rules with complete control over all aspects of life and under which all opposition is banned

< 46 >

WEBSITES

Eight Jules Verne Inventions That Came True
http://news.nationalgeographic.com/news/2011/02/pictures/110208-jules-verne-google-doodle-183rd-birthday-anniversary/
National Geographic features eight objects invented by Verne that later became a reality.

Frankenstein: Penetrating the Secrets of Nature
http://www.nlm.nih.gov/exhibition/frankenstein/galvanism.html
Learn more about galvanism and other topics related to Mary Shelley's Frankenstein.

Ray Bradbury
http://www.raybradbury.com/index.html
Explore Ray Bradbury's official site and watch video clips from an interview conducted in 2001.

Science Channel: Prophets of Science Fiction
http://science.discovery.com/tv/prophets-of-science-fiction/
Watch short biographical videos about popular science fiction authors such as Robert Heinlein.

Every effort has been made to ensure that these sites are suitable for children, that they have educational value, and that they contain no inappropriate material. However, because of the nature of the Internet, it is impossible to guarantee that these sites will remain active indefinitely or that their contents will not be altered.

SELECTED BIBLIOGRAPHY

Barron, Neil, ed. *Anatomy of Wonder: A Critical Guide to Science Fiction*. New York: R. R. Bowker Company, 1987.

Cunningham, Jesse G., ed. *Science Fiction*. San Diego: Greenhaven Press, 2002.

Hartwell, David G., and Kathryn Cramer, eds. *The Ascent of Wonder: The Evolution of Hard SF*. New York: Tor, 1994.

———. *The Space Opera Renaissance*. New York: Tor, 2006.

Kelleghan, Fiona, ed. *Classics of Science Fiction and Fantasy Literature*. Pasadena, Calif.: Salem Press, 2002.

MacNee, Marie, ed. *Science Fiction, Fantasy, and Horror Writers*. 2 vols. New York: UXL, 1995.

Miller, Ron. *The History of Science Fiction*. New York: Franklin Watts, 2001.

Saricks, Joyce G. *The Readers' Advisory Guide to Genre Fiction*. Chicago: American Library Association, 2001.

< 47 >

< 48 >